Contents

Figures

Tables

Executive Summary

The Appalachian Region, as defined by Congress, stretches more than 1,000 miles from northeastern Mississippi to the southern tier of New York. Spanning 205,000 square miles in 420 counties across 13 states, Appalachia is home to 25 million people and to diverse economic, social, and natural landscapes.

The Appalachian Region confronts a combination of challenges that few other parts of the country face—mountainous terrain, dispersed population, environmental issues, and lack of financial and human capital. While the Region has a wide array of natural and human resources to meet these challenges, its rate of economic growth and development has not kept pace with that of the nation. This report provides a profile of the people, the economy, and the natural resources of the Appalachian Region.

The well-being of the Appalachian people, the core objective of any development strategy, remains below the national average on a vast range of key indicators, including employment and earnings levels, household income levels, poverty rates, and educational attainment. In addition, Appalachia has higher rates of serious disease, mortality, and disability than the nation as a whole, and in some areas of the Region it is difficult to access treatment and affordable health care. Some Appalachian communities also lack the physical infrastructure necessary to create robust, sustainable local economies, such as adequate water and sewer systems and broadband access.

Each subregion of Appalachia faces unique challenges. In Central Appalachia, persistent socioeconomic distress and out-migration have resulted in a significant gap in human, natural, and financial capital, which greatly hinders economic development. Northern Appalachia continues to work to overcome deindustrialization and depopulation, and to develop niche industries to restore stability to the regional economy. Southern Appalachia has generally enjoyed relatively high population and job growth over the past few decades due to its focus on preserving and enhancing its manufacturing-based economy.

The consistent contrast between regional and national measures of well-being is at odds with a region possessing abundant natural resources and enjoying significant locational advantages. The Region's large reserves of energy and water have provided a solid base for traditional industries such as farming, forestry, mining, and manufacturing. However, patterns in global trade and technology have shaken Appalachia's historic economic reliance on its natural resources and disrupted many local economies that were already fragile.

The combination of these special problems in Appalachia has resulted in concentrated areas of poverty and unemployment. And while the Region has a wealth of natural resources that have benefited the nation, those resources have not generated the level of economic stability, employment, and prosperity that is found across the rest of the nation.

The development of new strategies for the growth and diversification of Appalachia's economy must therefore account not only for the challenges and opportunities facing Appalachia, but also for the tremendous diversity of needs and assets across the Region.

I. The Appalachian Region

Appalachia encompasses a variety of urban and rural settlement patterns. Throughout this report, the metropolitan classification system approved by the U.S. Office of Management and Budget is frequently used to capture differences in "rural" and "urban" socioeconomic characteristics, with "metro" used interchangeably with "urban," and "nonmetro" used interchangeably with "rural."

Figure 1. Rural and Urban County Types in Appalachia

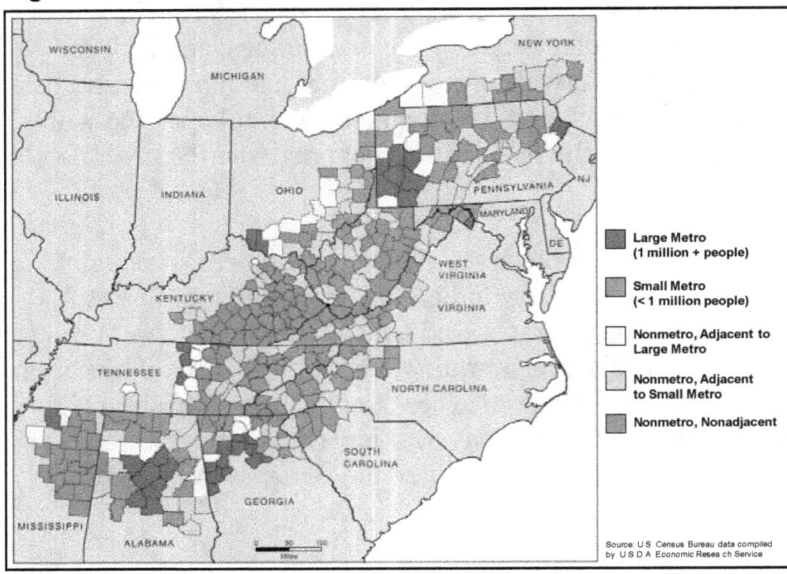

The Region includes all of two large metro areas (Pittsburgh and Birmingham) and parts of other large metro areas (notably, Cincinnati, Nashville, and Atlanta). Close to one-fourth of all Appalachians live in these major metro areas, but the proportion of the population living in rural and small town areas is much higher in Appalachia than in other parts of the country. Over 36% of the 25 million residents of Appalachia live in nonmetro counties, compared with 15% for the nation as a whole.

Figure 2. Appalachian Subregions

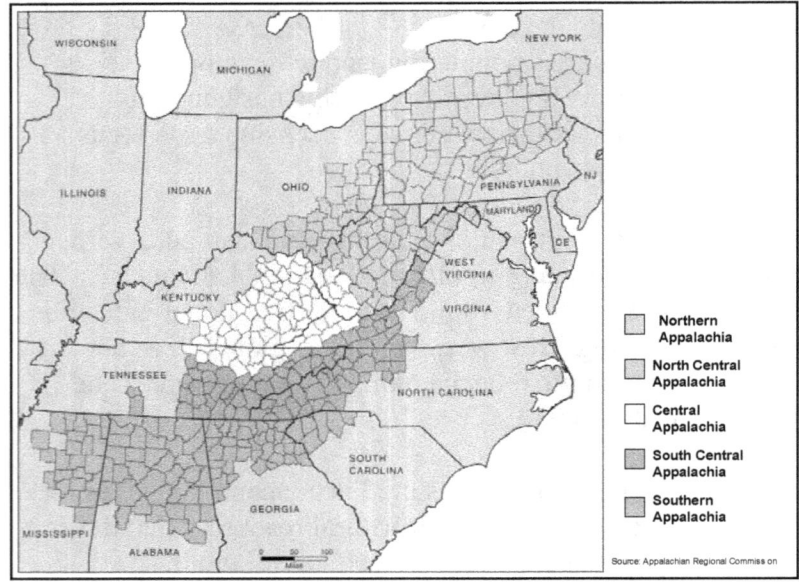

The Region has been divided by the Appalachian Regional Commission into five subregions—Northern Appalachia, North Central Appalachia, Central Appalachia, South Central Appalachia, and Southern Appalachia—according to common economic and demographic characteristics.

II. The People of Appalachia

The Appalachian Region has seen notable improvement in its living conditions in recent decades, but the Region still ranks below the national average in many quality-of-life measures. Appalachia's subregions are characterized by often-stark contrasts in the well-being of their populations: some communities have successfully diversified their economies and improved services, while others are still isolated and require basic educational and infrastructure improvements, such as roads and water and sewer systems.

The Region's isolation and the difficulties its communities have encountered in working to diversify their economies are major factors contributing to the gap in living standards and economic achievement between Appalachia and the rest of the nation. Many long-standing challenges remain, including persistently high rates of out-migration by the Region's youth, and below-average levels of education and income in some areas. Population out-migration remains well above the national average, and there is continuing concern about the decline in Appalachia's "prime age" workforce—workers between the ages of 25 and 55. Central Appalachia in particular still battles economic distress, with concentrated areas of high poverty, unemployment, poor health, and severe educational disparities.

Population

Appalachia's population in 2008 was nearly 25 million. The Region continues to grow more slowly than the rest of the nation, and within the Region, rates of population change are lower in counties that are rural and more isolated. From 2000 to 2008, Appalachia's population grew by 5%, compared with 8% for the nation as a whole. While metro areas in Appalachia grew by more than 7% during this period, nonmetro areas grew by less than 2%. Nonmetro counties in other parts of the country grew faster than those in Appalachia but still lagged considerably behind metro areas.

County population change in Appalachia between 2000 and 2008 ranged from a loss of nearly 17% (in McDowell County, West Virginia) to a gain of over 70% (in Forsyth County, Georgia). Over 40% of Appalachian counties lost population in that time period. In the rest of the nation, the vast majority of declining counties are nonmetro, but in Appalachia, 46 of the 185 declining counties are in metro areas. Declining and slow-growing counties dominate in western Pennsylvania, West Virginia (except the eastern panhandle), eastern Kentucky, and parts of Alabama and Mississippi. The fastest-growing counties are in the suburbanizing fringe of northern Atlanta and along the eastern edge of the Region, where once-rural counties are being affected by metropolitan expansion.

Counties in most parts of South and South Central Appalachia are growing at much higher rates than counties in Central Appalachia, which is more sparsely settled and less accessible. Most counties in North Central and Northern Appalachia either declined in population or grew modestly from 2000 to 2008. Northern Appalachia lost nearly 2% of its population from 2000 to 2008, while Southern Appalachia grew by 14% during the same period.

Figure 3. Population Change in Appalachia, by County, 2000–2008

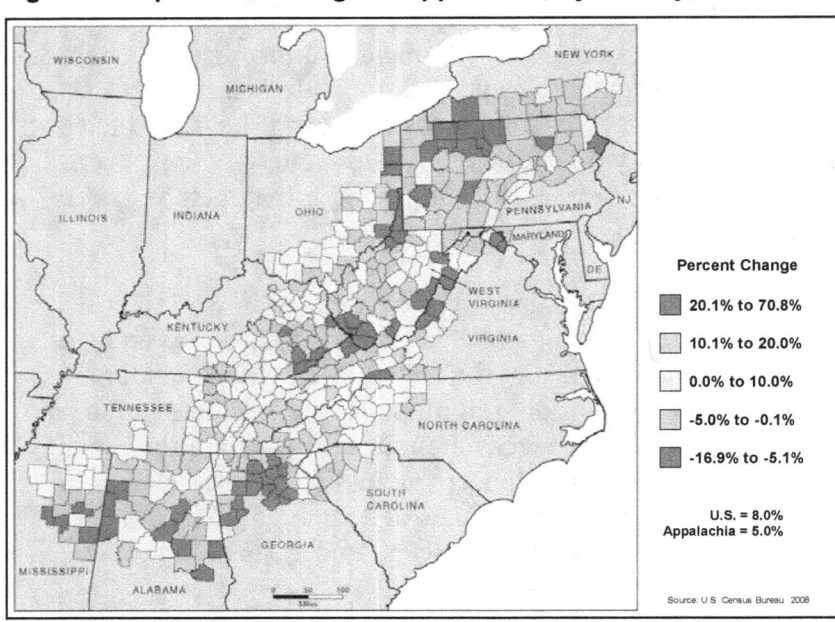

Percent Change

20.1% to 70.8%

10.1% to 20.0%

0.0% to 10.0%

-5.0% to -0.1%

-16.9% to -5.1%

U.S. = 8.0%
Appalachia = 5.0%

Source: U S Census Bureau 2008

Population change affects age structure and rural development prospects. The population profile of rural Appalachia is shifting: the percent of population in older age cohorts is increasing, partly as a result of age-specific migration patterns. In many parts of Appalachia, younger people are moving out, and in others, retirees are moving in. The population under age 25 in nonmetro counties in Appalachia declined by 5% at the same time the population age 65 and older grew by nearly 12%.

The rapid growth of the proportion of the population age 65 and older will likely continue, as baby boomers age into their retirement years and migrate in larger numbers to the more popular communities in the Region. Retirement-age population growth was over 21% in South Central Appalachia, compared with less than 7% in North Central and Northern Appalachia. Ongoing retiree in-migration to Southern and South Central Appalachia may be creating enough employment to cause much lower levels of out-migration among young adults in that subregion.

Table 1. Population Change in Appalachia, by Subregion and Age

Population, by Subregion			Percent Change, by Age, 2000–2008			
	Total, 2008 (thousands)	Change, 2000-2008 (thousands)	Total	Under Age 25	Age 25 to 64	Age 65 or Older
Appalachian Region	24,826	1,189	5.0	-5.0	4.4	11.9
Northern Appalachia	8,293	-155	-1.8	-7.8	2.1	6.5
North Central Appalachia	2,373	53	2.3	-7.1	2.9	6.9
Central Appalachia	1,914	25	1.3	-7.8	5.3	11.6
South Central Appalachia	4,612	322	7.5	0.1	6.4	21.3
Southern Appalachia	7,634	945	14.1	-0.9	6.8	17.2

Source: U.S. Census Bureau

Education

High educational attainment raises productivity, increases lifetime earning capacity, reduces poverty risk, and is highly correlated with a variety of measures of well-being. A region's educational attainment rate is one of the best long-term predictors of economic growth. The proportion of adults age 25 or over in Appalachia with a college degree is about two-thirds the national average, and the gap is widening. This phenomenon is partly due to college-educated young adults not returning to or settling in the Region, and partly due to a lower college-going rate among high school graduates in Appalachia. All Appalachian subregions lag behind the nation in college attendance and completion, but Central Appalachia has the lowest rates of educational attainment. Roughly 24% of Central Appalachians age 25 or older have attended college, compared with over half of the U.S. population age 25 or older.

Figure 4. High School Completion Rates in Appalachia, by County, 2000

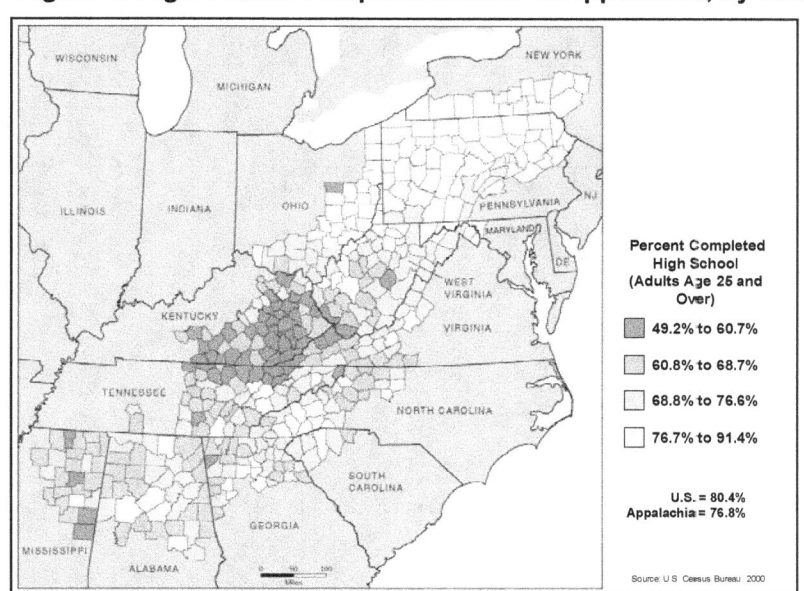

Figure 5. College Completion Rates in Appalachia, by County, 2000

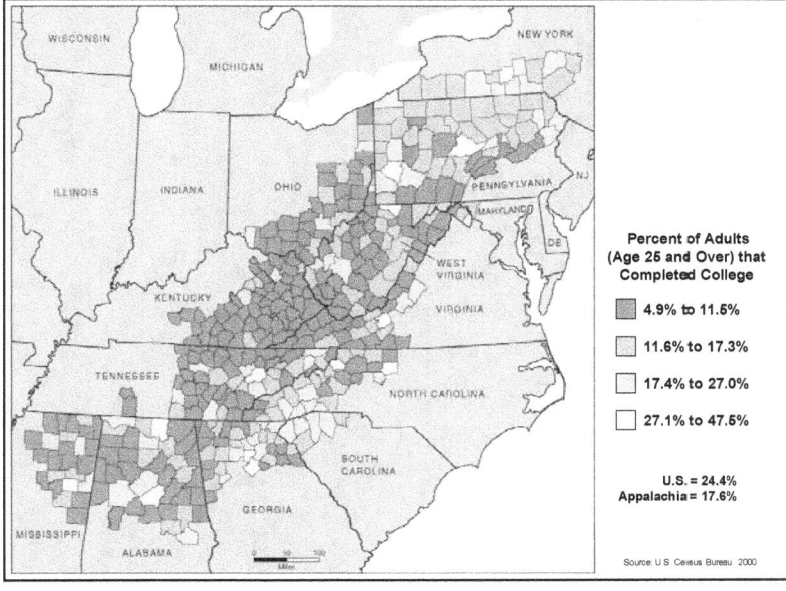

Health

Appalachia has higher rates of serious disease and mortality than the nation as a whole, and this problem is compounded by the lack of access to affordable care in some parts of the Region. Rates of cancer, heart disease, and diabetes in the Region exceed the national average. All Appalachian subregions had higher mortality rates than the nation during 2006 except Northern Appalachia, where mortality rates in both nonmetro and metro counties fell below the national rate. The mortality rate was highest in nonmetro Central Appalachia in 2006, with 1,035 deaths per 100,000 people. The nationwide mortality rate in 2006 was 830.8 deaths per 100,000 people. The percentage of adults with disabilities is another important measure of health conditions in Appalachia. Disabilities limit the scope of employment opportunities and often require publicly provided services. The proportion of Appalachians age 21 to 64 with a disability was 21.3% in 2000, compared with 19.2% for the nation as a whole. All Appalachian subregions except Northern Appalachia had higher disability rates than the national average. Central Appalachia had the highest rate, at 31.8%. Rural counties generally had higher disability rates than metro counties.

Table 2. Percent of Persons Age 21 to 64 with Disabilities

United States	19.2%
Appalachian Region	21.3%
Northern Appalachia	17.9%
North Central Appalachia	22.5%
Central Appalachia	31.8%
South Central Appalachia	22.0%
Southern Appalachia	21.4%

Compiled by the Appalachian Regional Commission; Source: U.S. Census Bureau; Census 2000

Figure 6. Disability Rates in Appalachia, by County, 2000

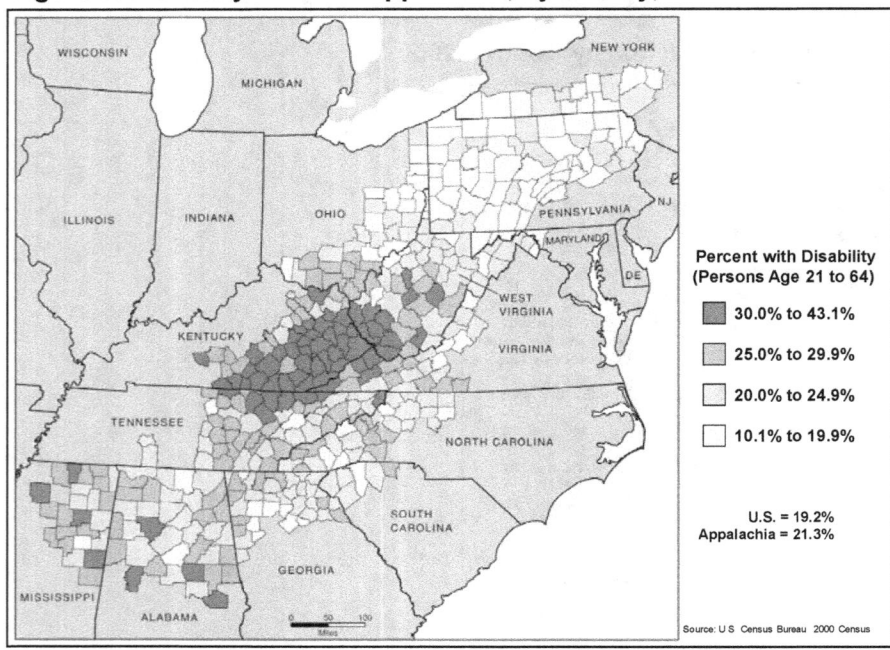

6

Poverty

In 1965, one in three Appalachians lived in poverty. In 2000, the poverty rate in Appalachia was 13%, only slightly above the U.S. average. Between 1965 and 2000, the number of counties with poverty rates greater than 1.5 times the U.S. average declined from 295 to 116. While high-poverty counties once spanned the entire Region, they are now largely concentrated in Central Appalachia.

Figure 7. High-Poverty Counties in Appalachia, 1960 and FY 2010
(Counties with Poverty Rates at Least 1.5 Times the National Average)

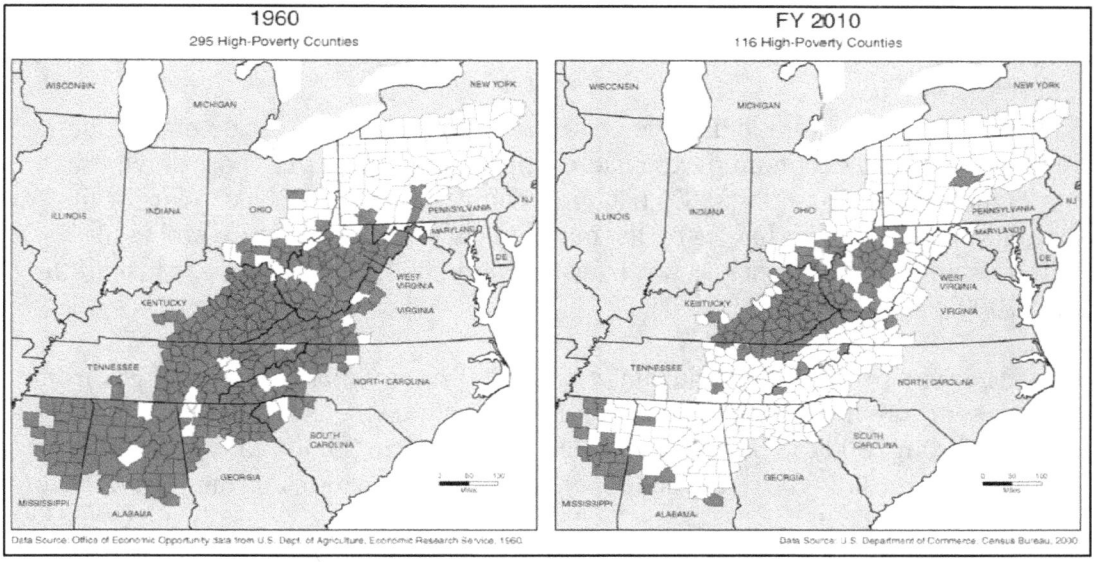

Appalachia's poverty rate is now higher than it was in 2000, an emerging trend that was intensified by the 2007–2009 economic recession. According to 2008 data from the U.S. Census Bureau's Small Area Income and Poverty Estimates program, 17.9% of Appalachia's residents live in poverty.

There is considerable geographic variation in poverty rates within Appalachia. In 2008, poverty rates were highest in Central Appalachia (24.6%) and lowest in Northern Appalachia, where poverty rates were only one percentage point higher than the national average. In all but one subregion, the average poverty rate for metro counties was lower than the rate for nonmetro counties. In South Central Appalachia, the average poverty rates for nonmetro and metro areas were roughly equal, at 14.6%. The gap between metro and nonmetro poverty rates in most subregions of Appalachia reflects a similar gap nationwide.

Figure 8. Average Poverty Rates in Appalachia, by County, 2008

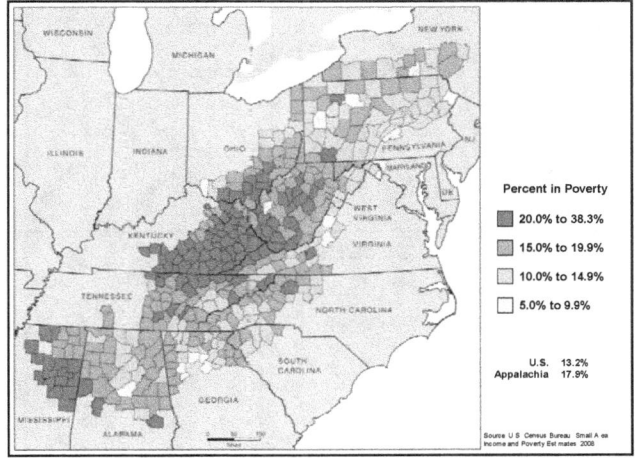

7

III. The Economy of Appalachia

Once highly dependent on mining, forestry, agriculture, and chemical and heavy industries, the Region's economy has become more diverse in recent times. Mining and manufacturing remain important industries in terms of economic output, but contribute a smaller share of jobs than they once did due to increased mechanization and outsourcing. While Southern Appalachia now has several auto manufacturing plants and a vast network of suppliers, traditional industries such as paper and wood products manufacturing have faced intense global competition and are in decline. The remarkable natural and human resources of Appalachia provide the potential for the development of diverse industries with substantial long-term economic, social, and environmental benefits.

In recent years, the Appalachian Region has been battered by job losses and structural economic changes. During the 2002–2007 economic expansion, employment increased more slowly in Appalachia than in the nation, averaging 0.8% per year, compared with 1.2% per year for the nation. The Region has also been hit harder by the current economic recession: while total employment in the nation has fallen back to levels last seen in 2004, Appalachia has lost all the jobs gained since 2000.

Job loss was most severe in Southern Appalachia, where total employment declined 9.2% from its 2007 peak; and less severe in Northern and Central Appalachia, where employment fell 4.6% over the same period. From 2000 to 2007, Appalachia lost more than 35,000 jobs in farming, forestry, and natural resources (8.8% of all such jobs), and 424,000 manufacturing jobs (22% of all such jobs).

Figure 9. Employment Growth in Appalachia and the Nation

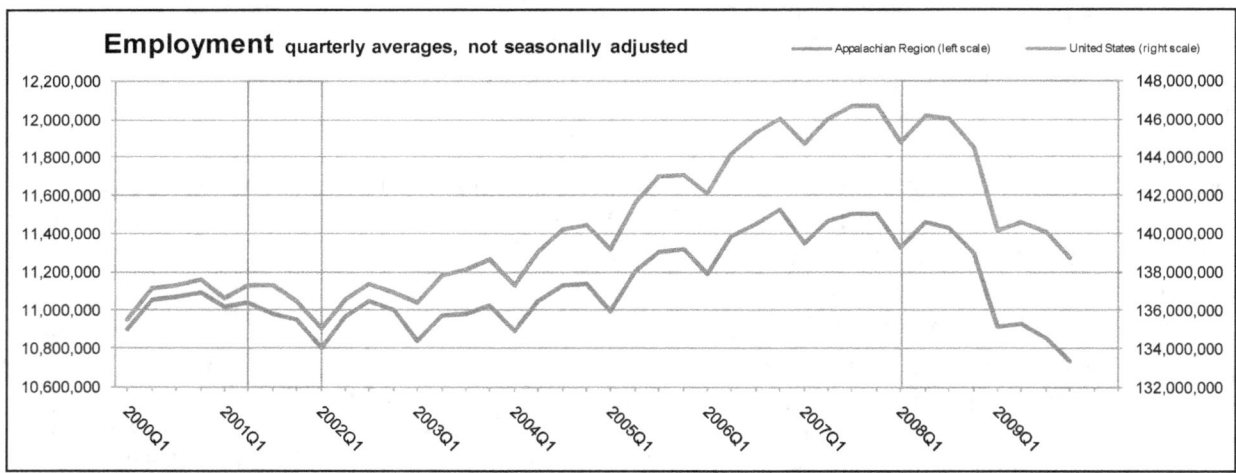

Source: Bureau of Labor Statistics

Figure 10. Average Annual Change in Employment in Appalachia, by Subregion

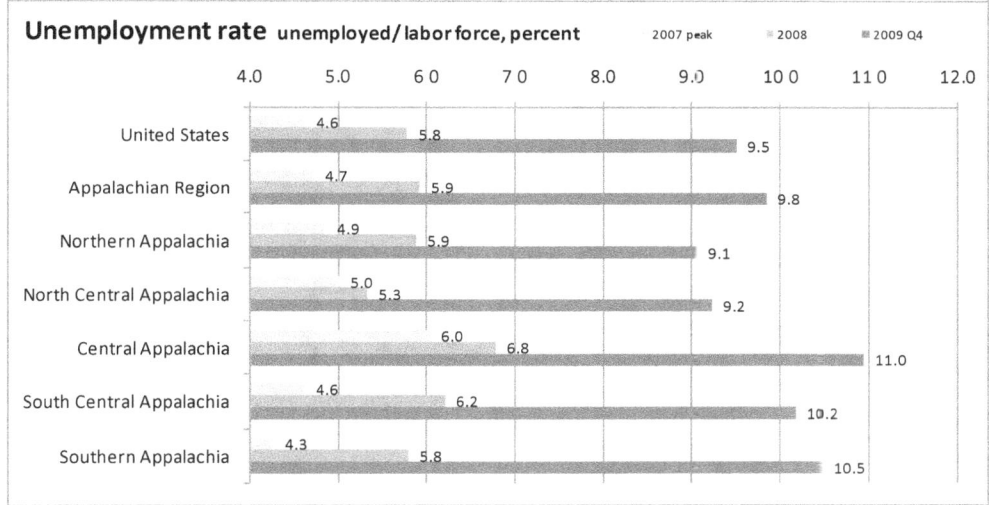

Employment average annual percent change ■2002q1-2008q1 expansion ■2007q4-2009q4 recession

	expansion	recession
United States	1.2	-5.5
Appalachian Region	0.8	-6.7
Northern Appalachia	0.3	-4.6
North Central Appalachia	0.7	-7.1
Central Appalachia	0.6	-4.6
South Central Appalachia	0.9	-6.7
Southern Appalachia	1.4	-9.2

Source: Bureau of Labor Statistics

Figure 11. Unemployment Rates in Appalachia, by Subregion

Unemployment rate unemployed/labor force, percent   2007 peak   ■2008   ■2009 Q4

	2007 peak	2008	2009 Q4
United States	4.6	5.8	9.5
Appalachian Region	4.7	5.9	9.8
Northern Appalachia	4.9	5.9	9.1
North Central Appalachia	5.0	5.3	9.2
Central Appalachia	6.0	6.8	11.0
South Central Appalachia	4.6	6.2	10.2
Southern Appalachia	4.3	5.8	10.5

Source: Bureau of Labor Statistics

Labor Force

During the 2002–2007 economic expansion, labor force growth was slower in Appalachia than in the nation, and during the recent recession, labor force contraction in the Region was much greater (-1.2% compared with -0.3%). The labor force declined most severely in Southern Appalachia (-3.0%) and in North Central Appalachia (-2.3%), where rates of manufacturing employment are very high. The proportion of the population that is employed, a measure of labor force participation, was 2 percentage points lower in Appalachia than in the nation as a whole in 2007 (45.8% and 47.8% respectively). While the employment-population ratio in most Appalachian subregions was close to the national average, the ratio in Central Appalachia was only 39.2%.

Unemployment

Unemployment rates measure the proportion of the labor force that is actively seeking employment but unable to find a job. The Appalachian Region's unemployment rate is generally higher than the rate for the nation as a whole. In the fourth quarter of 2009, the Region's unemployment rate was 9.8%, while the national rate was 9.5%. Nearly two-thirds of Appalachian counties have unemployment rates higher than the national average. However, the unemployment rate does not fully take into account the disproportionate share of Appalachian workers who left the labor force altogether as the economy contracted.

Unemployment trends in Appalachia closely tracked national trends during the 2000–2007 economic expansion and in the first year of the recession. In the fourth quarter of 2009, Central Appalachia's unemployment rate was 1.5 percentage points higher than the nation's, while the unemployment rates in Northern and North Central Appalachia were somewhat lower than the nation's.

Figure 12. Unemployment Rates in Appalachia, by County, Fourth Quarter 2009

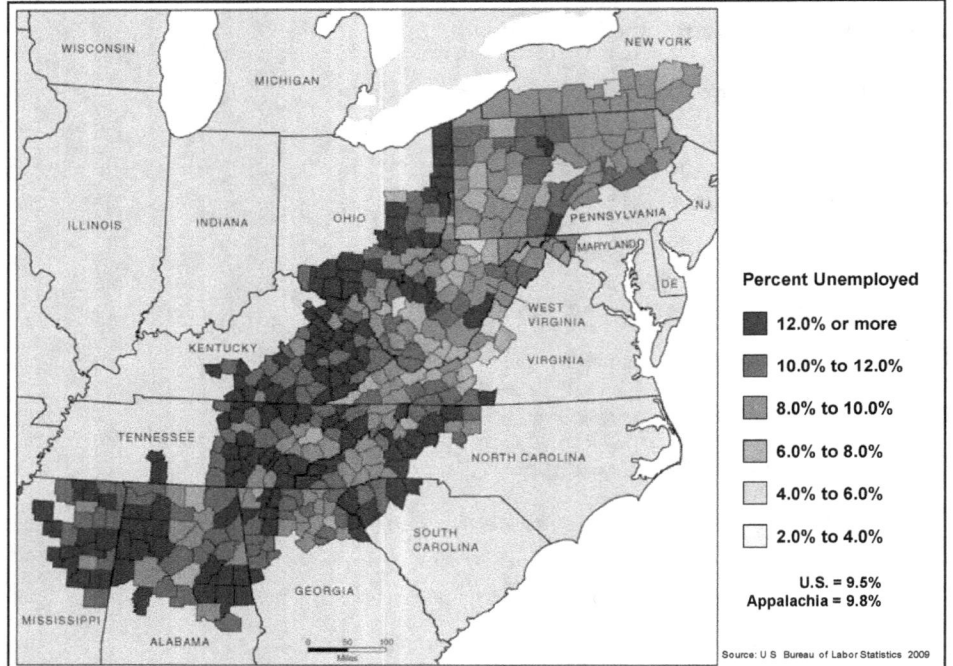

Industrial Composition

The Appalachian Region's industry concentration differs in important respects from the nation's. Industry concentration is the ratio of a sector's employment share in the Region to its employment share in the nation as a whole. The information services sector had the lowest employment concentration ratio among major industries in Appalachia in 2007, averaging .71. Between 2000 and 2007, employment in that sector fell 10% in Appalachia and 12.4% in the nation as a whole. The professional services sector also had a very low employment concentration in 2007, at .78, although it was among the fastest-growing sectors in Appalachia, with employment growth of 19.8% between 2000 and 2007. The employment concentration in the health and education sector ranged from .73 in Southern Appalachia to 1.32 in Northern Appalachia.

10

Typically, the manufacturing sector has been viewed as a source of relatively well-paid, stable employment opportunities. In the Region, manufacturing firms have looked to rural areas for relatively low-wage workers and favorable business climates in which to operate. However, structural changes in the industrial composition of the U.S. economy over the past decade have driven similar changes in Appalachia.

The Region's economy has historically been heavily dependent on mining, manufacturing, farming and natural resources, and utilities. In 2007, the mining sector had 1.6 times the national employment share, manufacturing had 1.4 times the national share, farming and national resources had 1.3 times the national share, and utilities had 1.25 times the national share. Most of these sectors experienced severe job losses between 2000 and 2007: manufacturing employment declined by 22%, utilities by 16%, and farming and natural resources by 8.8%.

Figure 13. Employment Change in Appalachia, by Industry, 2000–2007

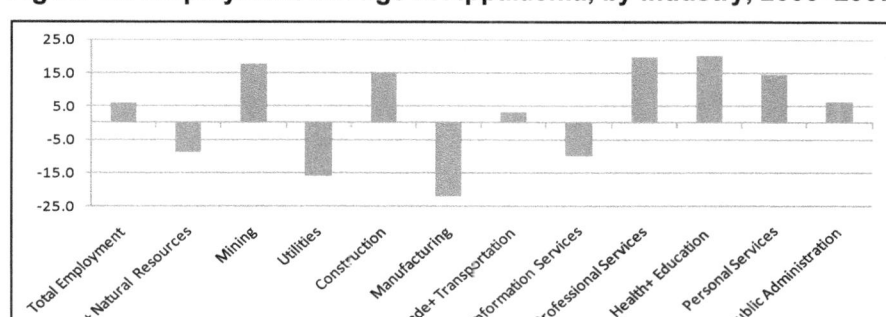

Source: Bureau of Economic Analysis

The sectors with the greatest job growth in Appalachia between 2000 and 2007 included health and education (20.1%), professional services (19.8%), mining (17.4%), construction (15%), and personal services (14.4%). However, all these sectors, with the exception of professional services, expanded at a slower rate in Appalachia than in the nation.

Figure 14. Employment Concentration in Appalachia, 2007

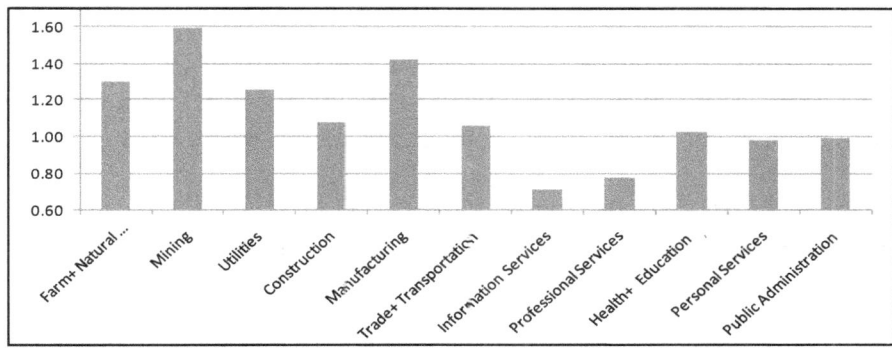

Source: Bureau of Economic Analysis

The information services sector is projected to continue adding the most jobs through 2015, although at a much slower rate in Appalachia than in the nation as a whole. Because this sector adds value and synergy to the overall economy and expands the productive capacity of the workforce, its relatively low concentration and growth rate in Appalachia could lead to a reduced capacity of the Region's workforce to compete in the global economy in the future.

11

Table 3. Employment Change and Concentration in Appalachia, by Industry and Subregion

Employment percent change 2000-2007	All Industries	Farm+ Natural Resources	Mining	Utilities	Construction	Manufacturing	Trade+ Transportation	Information Services	Professional Services	Health+ Education	Personal Services	Public Administration
United States	8.5	-7.8	27.6	-7.8	21.1	-18.6	4.9	-12.4	16.9	21.2	15.4	5.7
Appalachian Region	5.8	-8.8	17.4	-16.0	15.0	-21.9	3.1	-10.0	19.8	20.1	14.4	6.4
Northern Appalachia	1.8	-7.7	17.7	-31.7	9.5	-22.6	-0.1	-17.2	10.3	14.5	6.8	3.0
North Central Appalachia	4.9	-3.1	27.8	-7.7	11.7	-21.6	1.1	-16.9	13.0	16.6	13.9	2.2
Central Appalachia	3.9	-9.6	16.0	-23.3	9.6	-15.7	-1.4	12.5	14.7	17.1	14.6	3.3
South Central Appalachia	6.5	-13.7	6.2	-13.0	20.2	-27.6	4.3	5.3	23.4	28.9	18.1	6.6
Southern Appalachia	11.1	-7.5	6.8	4.0	18.7	-18.3	7.8	-10.2	30.8	28.2	22.1	13.0
	Total	**Industry concentration 2007**										
United States	180,944	1.00	1.00	1.00	1.00	1.00	1.00	1.00	1.00	1.00	1.00	1.00
Appalachian Region	13,250	1.30	1.59	1.25	1.08	1.42	1.05	0.71	0.78	1.02	0.98	0.99
Northern Appalachia	4,592	0.95	1.46	1.26	0.91	1.33	1.07	0.74	0.74	1.33	0.99	0.94
North Central Appalachia	1,160	1.75	4.10	2.40	1.04	0.94	1.03	0.71	0.66	1.09	1.01	1.23
Central Appalachia	828	3.48	7.89	1.06	1.03	1.19	1.03	0.72	0.56	0.93	0.87	1.16
South Central Appalachia	2,648	1.44	0.35	0.54	1.19	1.51	1.04	0.66	0.79	0.95	1.03	0.94
Southern Appalachia	4,022	1.03	0.53	1.43	1.22	1.66	1.07	0.71	0.88	0.73	0.94	0.99

Source: Bureau of Economic Analysis

Income

The Appalachian Region lags behind the nation in per capita personal income, a broad measure that includes wages and salaries; income from dividends, rent, and interest; and transfer receipts. Personal income less transfer payments is referred to as "market income." Per capita personal income was 20% lower in the Region than in the nation as a whole in 2007 ($29,274 compared with $36,601). Other forms of income are even lower in Appalachia relative to the nation. Per capita dividends, interest, and rent, and average proprietors' income (proprietors' income divided by number of proprietors) in Appalachia are 66% of the U.S. average.

There is a great deal of variation in per capita income among the Appalachian subregions. In 2007, Northern Appalachian counties had the highest average per capita personal income, at $29,396. Central Appalachian counties had the lowest, at $22,570. In Central Appalachia, dividends, interest, rent, and proprietors' income per capita were about half the U.S. average, while per capita personal income was 71% and per capita market income was only 61% of the U.S. average. As is true nationally, metro areas within the Appalachian Region had higher wages on average than nonmetro areas. The gap is especially large in Central and Southern Appalachia.

Per capita transfer payments were much higher in the Appalachian Region than in the nation as a whole in 2007, due to the Region's higher proportion of seniors and people with disabilities. (Transfer payments include Medicare, Medicaid, unemployment insurance, disability payments, personal injury claims, and net transfers from nonprofit institutions.) In 2007, per capita personal transfer payments were $5,388 in the nation as a whole and $6,185 in the Region. All Appalachian subregions exceeded the national average in 2007 except metro counties in Southern Appalachia. Transfer payments were highest in remote areas and areas with greater occupational hazards, such as the coalfields of Central Appalachia.

Disparities between Appalachia and the nation in per capita proprietors' earnings were more severe than disparities in other types of income. In Appalachian Kentucky and Virginia, per capita proprietors' earnings were 35% and 44% of the U.S. average in 2007, respectively. Proprietors' earnings were less than 75% of the U.S. average in the Appalachian portion of every state except Alabama, Pennsylvania, and West Virginia. Per capita income from dividends, interest, and rent in Appalachia was less than 75% of the national average in the Appalachian portion of every state except Alabama, Pennsylvania, and North Carolina.

Table 4. Personal Income, by Type

Per Capita Income Ratio to U.S.	United States 2000	United States 2007	Appalachia 2000	Appalachia 2007	Northern Appalachia 2000	Northern Appalachia 2007	Central Appalachia 2000	Central Appalachia 2007	Southern Appalachia 2000	Southern Appalachia 2007
Personal Income	1.00	1.00	0.81	0.80	0.87	0.87	0.71	0.71	0.83	0.80
Personal Transfer Payments	1.00	1.00	1.14	1.15	1.27	1.28	1.25	1.26	0.99	1.01
Personal Market Income	1.00	1.00	0.76	0.74	0.81	0.80	0.63	0.61	0.80	0.77
Dividends, Interest, and Rent	1.00	1.00	0.76	0.66	0.84	0.72	0.64	0.51	0.76	0.70
Net Earnings by Place of Residence	1.00	1.00	0.77	0.76	0.80	0.82	0.63	0.64	0.81	0.78
Contributions for Social Insurance	1.00	1.00	0.77	0.76	0.84	0.87	0.65	0.64	0.78	0.76
Earnings by Place of Work	1.00	1.00	0.72	0.72	0.79	0.80	0.57	0.58	0.76	0.73
Wage and Salary Disbursements	1.00	1.00	0.72	0.72	0.77	0.79	0.57	0.58	0.76	0.74
Wage and Salary Supplements	1.00	1.00	0.75	0.75	0.79	0.82	0.66	0.66	0.77	0.75
Proprietors' Income	1.00	1.00	0.71	0.66	0.88	0.85	0.50	0.48	0.72	0.65
Total Earnings Per Job	1.00	1.00	0.81	0.80	0.86	0.86	0.72	0.72	0.81	0.80
Wage and Salary Earnings Per Job	1.00	1.00	0.81	0.80	0.84	0.83	0.74	0.73	0.83	0.82
Wage and Salary Supplements Per Job	1.00	1.00	0.85	0.84	0.87	0.86	0.86	0.84	0.83	0.83
Proprietors Earnings Per Proprietor	1.00	1.00	0.75	0.73	0.98	0.99	0.53	0.55	0.72	0.67
Real Per Capita Income (2005 $)										
Personal Income	33,246	36,601	26,988	29,274	28,868	31,904	23,689	25,844	27,509	29,384
Personal Transfer Payments	4,278	5,388	4,862	6,185	5,421	6,919	5,342	6,811	4,236	5,444
Personal Market Income	28,968	31,213	22,126	23,089	23,448	24,985	18,347	19,033	23,272	23,941
Dividends, Interest, and Rent	6,064	6,416	4,583	4,252	5,084	4,623	3,880	3,254	4,628	4,518
Net Earnings by Place of Residence	22,903	24,797	17,543	18,837	18,364	20,361	14,468	15,779	18,645	19,423
Contributions for Social Insurance	2,770	3,035	2,125	2,321	2,329	2,652	1,796	1,951	2,166	2,304
Earnings by Place of Work	25,677	27,836	18,525	19,916	20,159	22,341	14,746	16,117	19,466	20,328
Wage and Salary Disbursements	19,050	19,995	13,664	14,317	14,650	15,827	10,830	11,528	14,528	14,780
Wage and Salary Supplements	3,743	4,557	2,802	3,418	2,957	3,730	2,473	3,025	2,876	3,424
Proprietors' Income	2,883	3,284	2,059	2,181	2,552	2,784	1,443	1,564	2,062	2,124
Total Earnings Per Job	43,448	46,350	35,031	37,071	37,476	39,878	31,186	33,403	35,219	36,942
Wage and Salary Earnings Per Job	38,672	41,600	31,395	33,463	32,622	34,605	28,459	30,424	31,906	34,041
Wage and Salary Supplements Per Job	7,599	9,482	6,438	7,988	6,585	8,156	6,499	7,983	6,315	7,885
Proprietors Earnings Per Proprietor	29,313	27,386	22,002	19,940	28,723	27,063	15,636	15,099	21,178	18,298

Source: Bureau of Economic Analysis

Note: Central Appalachia includes three of the five subregions referenced elsewhere in this report: North Central Appalachia, Central Appalachia, and South Central Appalachia.

Figure 15. Per Capita Market Income in Appalachia, by County, 2007

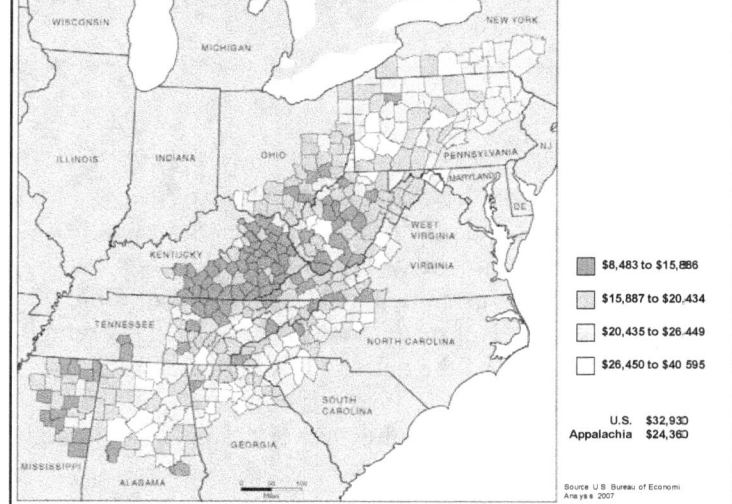

13

Job Skills and the "Creative Class"

Some occupational skills are thought to be more critical for maintaining economic competitiveness than others. One way to measure and compare occupational composition is to calculate the share of the workforce employed in the "creative class"—those workers who specialize in the novel combination of knowledge and ideas, such as engineers, designers, artists, business managers, and scientists. The share of the workforce employed in the creative class has been associated with higher rates of employment growth in both metro and nonmetro counties. In 2000, the creative class share in metro counties outside of Appalachia was nearly twice as large as the creative class share in metro counties in Central Appalachia. And nonmetro counties in Northern Appalachia had creative class shares at least as high as metro counties in Central Appalachia.

While creative class shares in metro counties in Southern Appalachia came closest to the non-Appalachian metro average, the 1990–2000 growth rate of creative class share lagged in all Appalachian subregions with the exception of Northern Appalachia. Nonmetro Appalachian counties in general appear to be nearing parity with nonmetro counties in the nation as a whole on this metric, but all nonmetro counties are falling farther behind metro counties. To the extent that growth in a knowledge-based economy is dependent on discovery and exploration of novel products and ideas, the lack of workers specialized in these tasks in Appalachia suggests a possible barrier to growth.

Table 5. Creative Class Share of Total Employment in Appalachia, by County Type

	Metro Counties			Nonmetro Counties		
	2000	1990	Growth	2000	1990	Growth
Non-Appalachian	24.9%	17.9%	39.1%	13.7%	11.7%	17.1%
Appalachian	19.8%	15.0%	32.0%	12.2%	10.2%	19.6%
Northern Appalachia	18.9%	13.6%	39.0%	12.9%	11.0%	17.3%
North Central Appalachia	17.9%	14.6%	22.6%	12.1%	10.2%	18.6%
Central Appalachia	12.5%	10.7%	16.8%	10.7%	8.7%	23.0%
South Central Appalachia	18.5%	15.4%	20.1%	12.2%	10.4%	17.3%
Southern Appalachia	22.1%	17.2%	28.5%	12.2%	9.7%	25.8%

Source: EEOC Special Tabulations of the U.S. Census

Infrastructure

Appalachian communities need adequate infrastructure in order to take full advantage of the emerging economic recovery and create robust, sustainable local economies. The development of highways and infrastructure such as water and wastewater treatment systems and broadband communications networks is one of the best ways to equip communities with the basic "building blocks" essential for economic and community development. But many significant challenges remain before the Region's infrastructure is at full parity with the rest of the nation. Twenty percent of Appalachian households still do not have access to community water systems, compared with 10% nationwide. And 47% of Appalachian households are not served by public sewer systems, compared

14

with a national average of 24%. In addition, Appalachia lacks a sufficient system of intermodal facilities and inland ports to compete successfully in global markets.

Broadband, or high-speed, access to the Internet also strengthens the rural and regional economy by increasing productivity, reducing costs, and enabling business, government, and personal activities to shift to the Internet. Broadband also supports distance learning and telemedicine applications, and helps small businesses enter the world of e-commerce. These activities have particular value for rural, more isolated communities that do not have the same level of access more densely populated areas do. Population, employment, and earnings growth are higher in communities with greater broadband availability. While the Internet has become widely available, high-speed internet access has been less prevalent in rural areas such as Appalachia. Underserved and unserved areas still exist, but they have greatly diminished in number in recent years, including in Appalachia.

IV. The Natural Resources of Appalachia

The Appalachian Region's rich and varied natural resources—forests, water, soils, energy, and minerals—have contributed greatly to its economic development and drive a significant share of its economic activity. The range of the Region's topography, from the steep hills and mountains that cover much of the Region to the broad river valleys of Southern Appalachia, is matched by great variety in climate, soils, and mineral wealth.

Water

Much of the Appalachian Region is characterized by the cool-moist-temperate climate-associated with higher elevations. The temperate climate produces large volumes of fresh water and abundant, high-quality hardwood. The Region includes the headwaters of most major eastern rivers, with many downstream communities dependent on streams flowing from Appalachia, many of which originate on federal lands. Forested watersheds provide water purification, mitigation of floods and droughts, soil retention, and maintenance of habitats. Surface runoff is rare in forest environments, as most rainfall moves to streams through subsurface flows where nutrient uptake, cycling, and contaminant absorption processes are rapid. Because of the dominance of subsurface flow, peak flows are moderated and base flows are prolonged. The quality and abundance of fresh water in streams and rivers result in great aquatic species biodiversity.

Figure 16. Mean Annual Water Supply in Appalachia

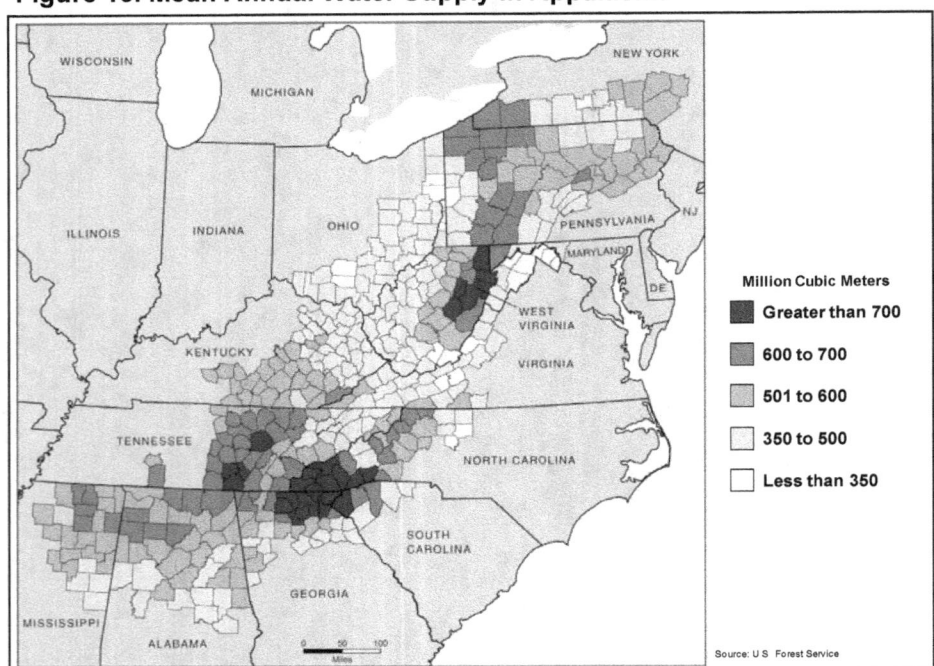

Appalachia's aquatic resources face significant threats to water quality and flow from inadequately treated sewage and industrial waste. Roughly half of Appalachian households are not served by public sewer systems. Streams once used for swimming, fishing, and drinking water have been adversely affected, and groundwater resources used for drinking water have been contaminated. In some areas, forest lands that sustain water quality and habitat have been

16

fragmented or lost. Much attention has been given to the link between water quality and mountaintop mining, which has buried nearly 2,000 miles of Appalachian streams. (See *The Effects of Mountaintop Mines and Valley Fills on Aquatic Ecosystems of the Central Appalachian Coalfields*, U.S. Environmental Protection Agency, December 2009; *EPA Issues Comprehensive Guidance to Protect Appalachian Communities from Harmful Environmental Impacts of Mountaintop Mining*, U.S. Environmental Protection Agency, April 2010; and "Mountaintop Mining Consequences," *Science* Magazine, January 8, 2010.)

Forests

Forests are a critical natural resource that shaped the Region's history and influenced its culture. Nearly all of the Region's forest land experienced intensive timber harvesting and deforestation during the late 1800s and early 1900s. These resilient forests today cover 86 million acres (65% of the Region), providing wildlife habitat and recreation, protecting the Region's waters, and supporting an extensive wood products industry. Over the last half-century the Region has gained considerable amounts of forest area as agricultural lands reverted to forest. This trend has slowed in recent years, and overall the Region's total amount of forest area can be described as stable, with gains nearly equal to losses.

The physical characteristics of climate, topography, and water resources in the Region result in a diverse and highly productive forest ecosystem. There are about 25 softwood tree species and 100 hardwood species of commercial importance growing in the Region, as well as numerous species of herbaceous plants, shrubs, and other tree species. This diversity of plant life provides a variety of habitats for birds and other wildlife species, which attracts bird watchers, hikers, and campers. The Region is recognized for its exceptional species diversity, but a number of species are at risk. The Region's ecosystem—scenic topography, forest cover, abundant fresh water, and wildlife and their habitats—provides substantial opportunities for tourism and recreation.

Nearly all of the Region's forest land is considered timberland—land that is potentially available to produce crops of timber. The Region contains 514 billion board feet of timber, 83% of which is hardwood and amounts to a third of the nation's hardwood resources. Many of the species growing in the Appalachian Region are prized by the hardwood lumber industry. The Allegheny Plateau of Pennsylvania and New York is home to two-thirds of the nation's black cherry resources. The Region also has 33% of the nation's sugar maple sawtimber volume, 54% of the yellow-poplar volume, 36% of the red maple volume, and 36% of the oak volume. Nearly half of the Region's hardwood sawtimber volume is in the more valuable and preferred grade 1and 2 trees.

The Appalachian Region's working forests are maturing, with increasing stand size, tree size, and density. Sixty-two percent of stands are dominated by large-diameter trees, and most stands are well stocked, although much of the Region has the potential to produce greater volumes of wood with better management. Nearly half of the large-diameter trees are species of oak, yet oak regeneration is lagging maple regeneration. This successional change in species composition will affect the timber industry as well as wildlife habitats.

Figure 17. Ownership of Forest Land in Appalachia

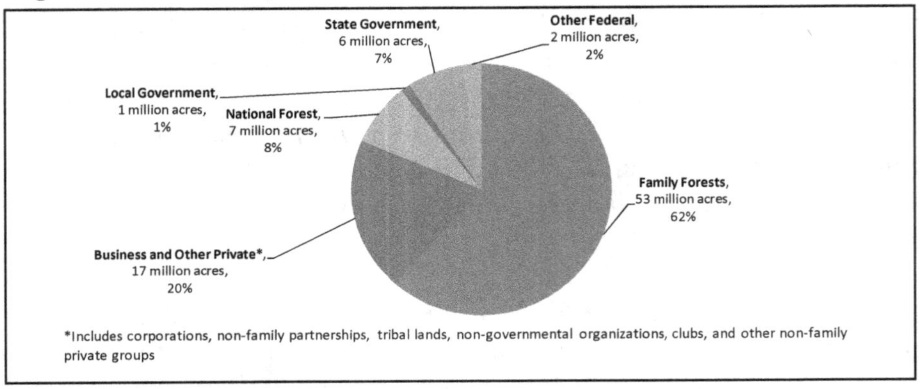

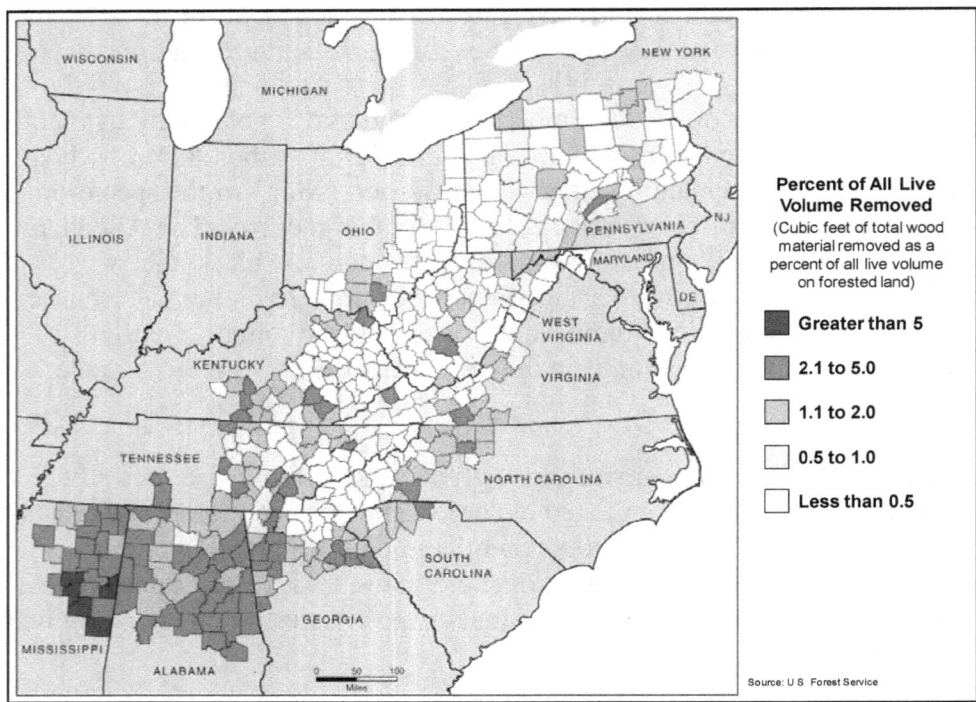

Source: USDA Forest Service, Forest Inventory and Analysis program

Appalachian forests are growing nearly twice as much wood as is being harvested. Forests are growing at an annual rate of 3% of current inventory, and of this, 1.7% is removed each year for all purposes, leaving a surplus of growth to accumulate in the forest. Ratios of growth to removals indicate that current harvesting is at sustainable levels and that there is potential for increased rates of harvesting. Four out of every five acres of forestland in the Appalachian Region are in private ownership, and most of these private holdings are family forests. Family forests are generally small and are held for reasons other than timber production. To a large extent, the sustainability of the Region's forests and the benefits they provide rest in the hands of these numerous private owners.

Figure 18. Wood Harvest Intensity in Appalachia

Biomass

As domestic demand for hardwood lumber from furniture and other secondary wood products manufacturers has declined, hardwood lumber manufacturers must increasingly compete in global markets. While exports of hardwood lumber have compensated for some of the decline in domestic markets, emerging markets for biomass (organic matter derived from trees and grasses) offer a new economic opportunity for the Appalachian Region. Appalachian timberland contains an estimated 4.6 billion dry tons of standing above-ground biomass, nearly one-fifth of all the aboveground biomass in the United States. Over a third of the biomass is growing in stands classified as below full density, enabling current income opportunities as well as long-term improvements in stand productivity.

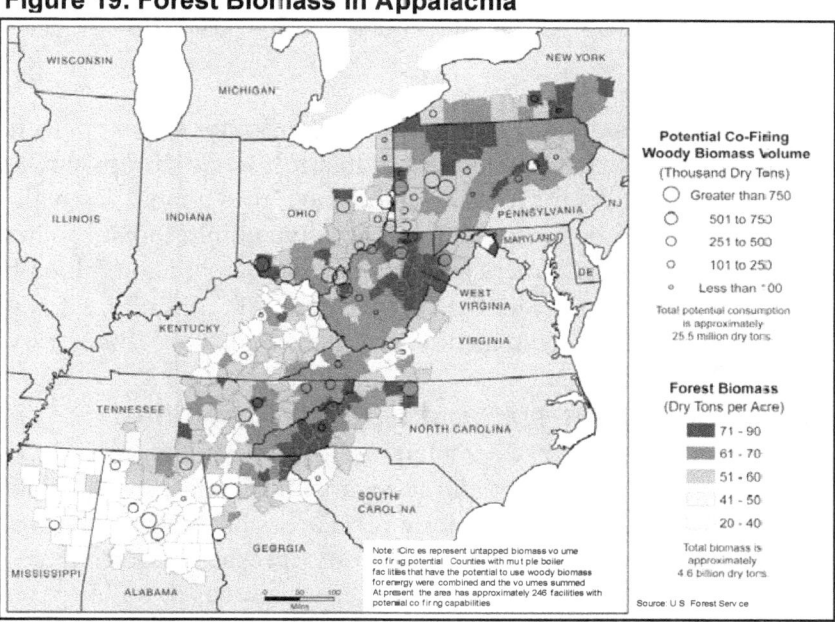

Figure 19. Forest Biomass in Appalachia

While 2.5 million truckloads of biomass are harvested in the Region each year, an estimated 585,000 truckloads of recoverable material are left in the woods as logging residue, which could be recovered with increased operational efficiency and/or investments in newer technology. Much of this material could be removed without sacrificing the ecosystem services provided by decaying woody material on the forest floor. In addition, 26.4 million cubic feet of mill residue remains unused each year, produced by numerous small sawmills that dominate the Region.

One emerging market for Appalachia's forest resources is the use of woody biomass for co-firing with traditional coal-fired energy production. Ultimately, an annual positive net change in standing inventory, coupled with biomass growing in understocked stands and unused logging and mill residue, offers important resources to an emerging woody biomass industry while maintaining current traditional forest products markets.

Timber

The Appalachian Region produces 13% of the nation's total timber product output volume. In 2007, 1.9 billion cubic feet of roundwood products were harvested in the Region, enough to build 557,000 new homes. Since 2004, the Region's total timber product output volume has declined approximately 9%, and further declines are expected. While there are 1,005 primary wood processing mills in the Region, they represent a small fraction of the number of mills and processing capacity that once existed. Although Appalachia continues to produce and export high-quality hardwood products and timber, some of which are prized worldwide, the Region could benefit by increasing value-added processing.

Non-Timber Forest Products

Non-timber forest products are critical for the economic and ecological sustainability of the Appalachian Region. A dynamic medicinal herb industry, based on the Region's native forest plants, has existed in Appalachia since European immigrants first settled there in the mid 1700s. The industry continues to thrive, as the Region's vast floral diversity produces a cornucopia of plants with therapeutic uses. Over 150 Appalachian native plant species have medicinal value. Two-thirds of the American ginseng harvested from forests in the eastern United States comes from Appalachia.

There are well-established markets for plants native to Appalachia for the culinary, floral, decorative, landscaping, and craft industries. Civic groups throughout the Region generate significant revenues for local communities from annual festivals celebrating native Appalachian plants, including the ramp, which is a native edible forest product. A small but growing number of family forest landowners are growing medicinal and edible plants that generate income and improve forest health. The U.S. Department of Agriculture's National Agroforestry Center has efforts under way to evaluate the potential to produce understory plants with economic value.

Recreation, Tourism, and Natural Amenities

Nature-based recreation dependent on forest and other natural resources is important to the Appalachian Region. The natural beauty and climate of Appalachia have implications for long-term regional development. Many rural areas have attracted tourists and generated new jobs for people who enjoy the outdoors. Millions of residents participate in a variety of outdoor activities, and the proximity of the Region's recreation areas to major population centers makes them destinations for visitors from outside the Region, underscoring the importance of public lands and forests for Appalachia's economic development.

Soils and Land Use

The Appalachian Region contains a wide variety of soil landscapes. The glaciated plateaus and till plains of southern New York, northwestern Pennsylvania, and northeastern Ohio are characterized by nearly level to slightly rolling plains. Cropland is the dominant land cover on about 4.3 million acres, mostly composed of hay and pasture, corn, and small grains. Truck crops, orchards, and specialty crops like vineyards are also important to the Region. Hardwood and coniferous forests cover nearly three-fifths of Appalachia.

The lands in the agricultural areas of southwestern Ohio, central Kentucky, central Tennessee, and extreme northern Alabama are predominantly level or gently rolling hills. Cultivated agriculture accounts for about a tenth of the area, with crops mostly consisting of corn, soybeans, and other small grains, while specialty crops like tobacco, sorghum, winter wheat, and orchards trees are also important. Hardwood forests are found in small woodlots and more steeply sloping areas, and amount to about 43% of the land in this area. Development pressures are strong around metropolitan areas, including Atlanta, Cincinnati, Lexington, and Nashville.

The Allegheny and Cumberland Plateaus stretch from northern Alabama through Tennessee, Kentucky, Virginia, Ohio, West Virginia, Maryland, and Pennsylvania and into southwestern New York, and are deeply dissected by rivers and streams. The soils and topography of the area are generally unsuited for agriculture, with only 3.3% of the area under cultivation. Hay and pasture cover an additional tenth of the area, and support a viable livestock industry. Fruits and vegetables are important locally. The area supports a strong timber industry, with large areas of mixed hardwood forest on 70% of the total area.

The Ridge and Valley and Blue Ridge areas run from Alabama northeast through Pennsylvania. Both areas are characterized by level to gently sloping valleys separated by high parallel ridges. The valley floors are dominated by soils derived from limestone and shale parent materials that are high in natural fertility. Cultivated crops consist mainly of corn, soybeans, and small grains. Other important crops are potatoes, orchard fruits, and tobacco. The ridges and side slopes are mostly forested and support a good timber industry.

The Piedmont area of Appalachia touches a small part of southwest Virginia and runs south through North and South Carolina, Georgia, Alabama, and Mississippi. The topography in the area ranges from the steep slopes of the Blue Ridge to rolling hills dissected by meandering stream channels. The dominant geology is igneous and metamorphic, and the soils derived from these parent materials support a strong agricultural base, including corn, soybeans, and forage crops. Cotton is important in Mississippi and Alabama. Pasture and hay are grown on 16% of the land in these areas, while forest occupies about half of total acreage, mostly on steeper land.

Figure 20. Soil Landscape Regions in Appalachia

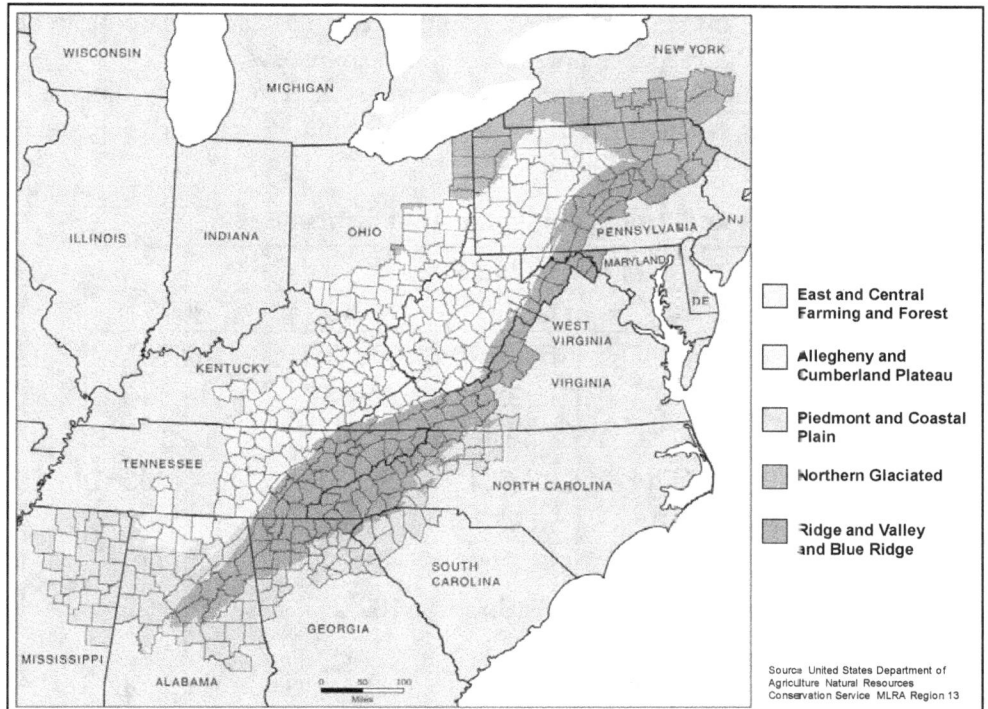

Energy: Oil and Natural Gas

The first well drilled in United States to obtain natural gas was drilled by William Hart in 1825 in Fredonia, New York. The modern petroleum industry began in 1859 when Colonel Edwin Drake produced oil from a well drilled to a depth of 69 feet near Titusville, Pennsylvania. Both towns are located in the Appalachian Region. The success of Drake's well ignited an "industrial explosion" that spread rapidly throughout the Region. Coal, oil, and natural gas are the principal fossil fuels produced in the Appalachian Basin and the Black Warrior Basin. They are non-renewable fuels: once they are mined or extracted, they will not be replaced.

Oil and natural gas are produced from Paleozoic strata 544 to 248 million years old. Current estimates of recoverable oil and natural gas in the basin are about 4.76 billion barrels of oil (BBO) and natural gas liquids, and 126 trillion cubic feet (TCF) of natural

Table 6. Hydrocarbon Resources in the Appalachian Basin

	Million Barrels of Oil and Natural Gas Liquids	Billion Cubic Feet of Gas
Produced	3,500	45,000
Undiscovered	927	70,290
Proven Reserves	329	106,000
Ultimate Recovery	4,756	125,890

Source: Energy Information Administration

gas. However, some industry sources have estimated that as much as 363 TCF of natural gas may be recoverable (see U.S. Geological Survey, May 2009). Of this amount, 3.5 BBO and 45 TCF have been produced. Proven reserves of oil and gas—the amounts identified and remaining to be produced—are 0.329 BBO and 10.6 TCF, respectively. The technically recoverable undiscovered oil and gas resources of the Appalachian Basin were assessed in 2002 by the U.S. Geological Survey as about 0.927 BBO, including natural gas liquids, and 70.29 TCF (statistical mean values).

Table 7. Natural Gas Gross Withdrawals and Production in the Appalachian Basin

	Million Cubic Feet				
	2004	2005	2006	2007	2008
Alabama (onshore)	173,106	164,304	160,381	155,167	152,051
Kentucky	94,259	92,795	95,320	95,437	114,116
Maryland	34	46	48	35	28
Mississippi	176,329	189,371	212,081	272,878	346,465
New York	46,050	55,180	55,980	54,942	50,320
Ohio	90,476	83,523	86,315	88,095	84,858
Pennsylvania	197,217	168,501	175,950	182,277	198,295
Tennessee	2,100	2,200	2,663	3,942	4,700
Virginia	85,508	88,610	103,027	112,057	128,454
West Virginia	197,217	221,108	225,530	231,184	245,578

Source: Energy Information Administration

Table 8. Crude Oil Proved Reserves and Production in the Appalachian Basin

	Million Barrels				
	2004	2005	2006	2007	2008
Alabama	5	5	5	5	5
Kentucky	2	2	2	2	1
Mississippi	17	18	15	22	21
Ohio	5	4	4	4	4
Pennsylvania	2	2	2	2	2
West Virginia	1	1	2	2	2

Source: Energy Information Administration

Between 1956 and 2007, annual Appalachian oil production declined from about 35.6 million barrels to 12.8 million barrels, worth about $909 million annually at the January 2010 price of $71 per barrel. During the same period, annual natural gas production increased from about 420 to 897 billion cubic feet, which at $10 per 1,000 cubic feet is valued at almost $9 billion. Although much of the Appalachian Region's original hydrocarbon resource has been extracted during the last 150 years, it is estimated that about 56% of the original gas resource and about 20% of the original oil resource remain to be discovered.

Future production of natural gas in the Appalachian Basin will come from shale deposits that are rich in organic matter, such as the Marcellus Shale in New York, Pennsylvania, and West Virginia; the Ohio shale in Kentucky; and tight gas sands in the northern Appalachian Basin; as well as from coal beds in Pennsylvania, West Virginia, Virginia, and Alabama. Drilling in these shale deposits is beginning to create significant economic growth and environmental impacts for energy-development companies and landowners.

Energy: Coal

Bituminous coal of the Triassic Age (248 million–213 million years old) was first extracted from the Richmond Basin, near Richmond, Virginia, by early Huguenot settlers in about 1703. Coal mining gradually developed on a large scale after the Civil War, at first near major centers of population. Mines were opened in more remote regions throughout Appalachia as the transportation infrastructure developed.

Appalachian anthracite from eastern Pennsylvania was first marketed as a clean-burning, hot coal, and was the fuel of choice for railroads, industry, and home heating during the early decades of the past century, before being replaced by cleaner-burning natural gas. Bituminous coal is still mined

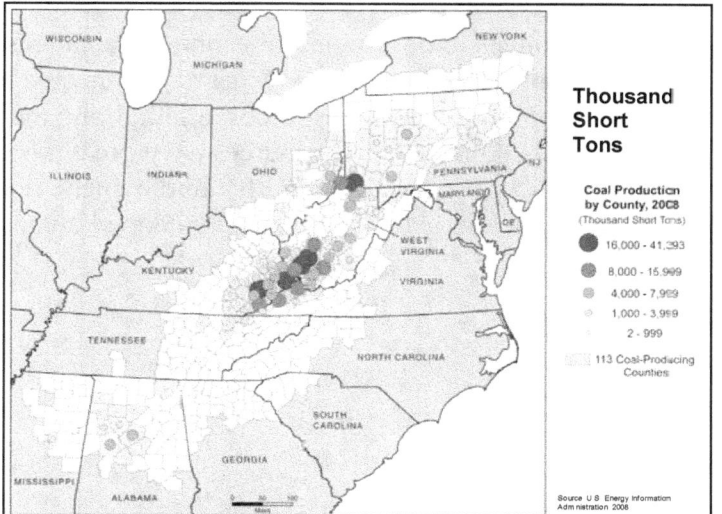

Figure 21. Coal Production in Appalachia, by County, 2008

extensively from Pennsylvania to Alabama for the electric power generation and for industrial purposes. Central Appalachia contains some of the best quality low-sulfur bituminous coal in the country.

Appalachian coal production peaked around 1998, and production from western states surpassed Appalachian production at about the same time. The Appalachian Basin currently supplies about 35%, or 390 million short tons (354 metric tons), of the 1.1 billion tons (998 metric tons) of coal mined each year in the United States. At the January 2010 average spot price of $56 per short ton, annual Appalachian Basin coal production was valued at about $22 billion. Coal mining in Appalachia is likely to continue for several decades, although mine productivity is declining as thicker, more accessible coal beds are mined out and succeeded by thinner and less-accessible coal seams.

The Appalachian counties that produce the most coal also have poverty and disability rates that are well above national and Appalachian averages. The fact that such great wealth has been produced in counties with such high rates of poverty and disability is an anomaly that merits further analysis.

Table 9. Poverty and Disability Rate Averages for U.S. Counties, Appalachian Counties, and Appalachian Coal-Producing Counties, 2008

	Poverty Rate	*Disability Rate*
United States (All Counties)	13.20%	19.2%
Appalachia (All Counties)	17.90%	21.3%
Appalachian Coal-Producing Counties	19.50%	48.3%
Top 10 Appalachian Coal-Producing Counties	22.60%	59.1%

Sources: Energy Information Administration; U.S. Census Bureau, Small Area Income and Poverty Estimates 2008

Conclusion

Appalachia continues to be a region of economic challenges. Its high rates of unemployment, disability, and poverty, along with low per capita income and college graduation rates, occur in a region with a wealth of natural resources, highlighting the need for economic diversification in the Region. While Appalachia's resources have greatly benefited the nation, they have not generated the level of economic stability, employment, and prosperity that one might expect from a region so rich in natural assets and untapped human potential.